Index

Abuse of Posit...
Access to Perso...
Action Plan Ord...
Adoption ....
Alcohol...2, 12, 28, 41
Anti-Social Behaviour Order.............................. 15
Armed Forces 28, 41
Arrest (see Police Detention)............................. 17
Attendance Centre 15, 24
Babysitting 2
Betting 41
Blood Donation 37
Borrowing Money.. 3
Care Order.. 37
Child Safety Order 3
Cinema.................................... 4, 12, 20, 26, 41
Community Service Order 28
Contact Order 4
Contraception 4
Contracts 5, 42

Councillor	46
Counselling	5
Criminal Liability	15
Cruelty to Child	29
Curfew Notice	5
Curfew Order	16
Custodial Sentence	24
Dental Treatment	29, 42
Detention and Training Order	26
Detention During Her Majesty's Pleasure	16
Detention for a Specified Period	17, 24
Driving Licence	29, 38, 42, 46
Emergency Protection Order	6
Evidence	6
Fares	13, 29
Fingerprints (see Police Detention)	17
Fireworks	42
Flying	38, 43
Fruit Machines	7
Gliding	30
Homelessness	30
Hypnotism	43
Jury Service	43
Leaving Alone	7
Leaving Care	32
Leaving Home	32
Marriage	32

Medical Treatment: Consent and Refusal	8, 32
Member of Parliament	46
Minimum Wage	44
Mortgage	44
Name Change	8, 34
Optical Treatment	34
Passport	8, 34
Performance	20, 35
Pet Purchase	21
Police:	
Detention	17
Powers of Protection	9
Premium Bonds	9
Prescription Charges	35
Prison	47
Probation Order	35
Prohibited Steps Order	9
Pubs	25
Rape / Unlawful Sexual Intercourse	18
Referral Order	18
Religion	10
Remand by a Court:	
To Local Authority Accommodation	19
To Secure Accommodation	21
Residence Order	10
Savings / Current Accounts	14

School Attendance	13, 36
Searches (see Police Detention)	17
Seatbelts	24
Section 8 (Children Act 1989) Orders	11
Secure Accommodation	22
Sexual Intercourse:	
Heterosexual	30
Homosexual	31
Smoking	11, 36
Solvents	44
Specific Issue Order	11
Supervision Order:	
Welfare	38
Criminal	19
Tattoo	44
Tissue / Body Donation	45
Truants – Power To Remove	13
Voting	45
Will	45
Work:	
Full-time	36
Part-time	19, 22, 25, 27
Youth Court	20

Introduction

This guide has been written for use by those adults and young people who wish to know at what age (in England and Wales) a child or young person is allowed by law to undertake, or be held responsible for a particular activity.

Like all other 'Personal Guides', it provides a simple yet accurate account of current legislation.

Readers can either consult the index where subjects are listed alphabetically or select a particular age from the following text to learn what rights and or responsibilities it brings with it.

Suggestions for additions to future editions are welcomed.

Appendix 1 contains details of some useful organisations concerned with age-related rights and responsibilities of children and young people, and appendix 2 a list of all Children Act Enterprises publications.

Child / Young Person of Any Age

In relation to some of the subjects covered below in the 'any age' section, the law does not specify a particular age of child or young person, or does not distinguish between them and adults.

Access to Personal Data

- At any age a child/young person can apply for access to personal data held in manual records or on computers.
- Regulations allow those who hold health, education or social work records some exemption from the obligation to provide access to the records if:
  - Serious harm to the mental or physical health or condition of the applicant or any other person would be likely if access were given [s.7 Data Protection Act 1998 and Data Protection (Subject Access Modification) Orders 2000)].

Alcohol - Confiscation

- If an under eighteen year old is found in a public place (or a private place where s/he has no right to be), consuming, or planning to consume alcohol the Police may confiscate it [s.1 Confiscation of Alcohol (Young Persons) Act 1997].

Babysitting

- There is no legal minimum age below which a child/young person may not lawfully baby-sit.
- Those who have parental responsibility for the child must ensure that the person they have asked to baby-sit is capable and will provide adequate care for the child

otherwise both those with parental responsibility and the babysitter risk prosecution for cruelty or neglect, or even a civil action.

NB. The NSPCC recommend sixteen as the minimum age for babysitting.

Borrowing Money

- There is no minimum age limit to borrow money.
- Potential lenders will be reluctant to risk their funds since any contract for repayment entered into by someone under eighteen is un-enforceable [s.1(b) Minor Contracts Act 1987].

Child Safety Order

- The 'child safety order' exists to protect children under ten at risk of becoming involved in crime and may require a child to be at home at certain times or to stay away from certain places or people [s.11 Crime & Disorder Act 1998].

Cinema

- At the discretion of the person/s who have parental responsibility for her/him a child/young person of any age can see a 'U' or 'PG' certificate film.

Contact Order (see also s.8 Order)

- If a court is satisfied that s/he has sufficient understanding, a child/young person of any age may be given leave (ie. permission of the court) to make an application for a 'contact order'[s.10 Children Act 1989].
- A contact order as defined in s.8 Children Act 1989 will determine with whom s/he has a right of contact.

Contraception

- There is no lower age limit to receive from G.P.s or family planning clinics contraceptive advice or treatment.
- Doctors do not have to inform parents. They will break confidentiality only if they believe a young person is being abused and even then they should normally inform the young person of their intentions.

Contracts

- A child of any age can theoretically enter into a valid contract for what are known as 'necessaries' eg. food and clothing and a job, but cannot enter into a legally binding agreement for goods or services in exchange for money [s.3 Minors' Contracts Act 1987].

Counselling

- There is no minimum age for the receipt of counselling (see also Medical Treatment.)

Curfew Notice

- Following consultation with local Police and other relevant people, a Local Authority can impose a 'child curfew notice' which for a maximum of ninety days:
  - Bans children and young persons aged less than sixteen from being in a public place within a specified area, during specified hours between 9pm and 6am unless they are under the effective control of a parent or responsible person aged eighteen or over [s.14 Crime and Disorder Act 1998 as amended by s.48 Criminal Justice and Police Act 2001].

Emergency Protection Order

- A child/young person of any age may for up to eight days be made subject of an 'emergency protection order' (a court order which authorises her/his removal from risk or detention in a safe place) if s/he is otherwise likely to suffer significant harm [s.44 Children Act 1989].

- It is unlikely that a court would grant an order on a young person of seventeen (or one of sixteen who is married) since once the order expires the Local Authority would not be able to seek to get the young person committed to their care.

Evidence

- In criminal proceedings a child is assumed to be a competent witness and her/his evidence is accepted unsworn [s.33A Criminal Justice Act 1988 inserted by sch.9 para.33 Criminal Justice and Public Order Act 1994].

NB. Eligible witnesses aged less than seventeen at the time of a trial are entitled to special measures to support them [ss.16 & 17 Youth Justice and Criminal Evidence Act 1999].

- In civil cases sworn evidence may be heard if the court is satisfied that the child understands its meaning, or unsworn evidence may be accepted if the court is satisfied that the child understands that s/he has a duty to tell the truth and has sufficient understanding to justify the evidence being heard [s.96 Children Act 1989].

Fruit Machines

- There is no minimum age to legally play fruit / gaming machines.

Leaving Alone

- There is no minimum age below which it is unlawful to leave a child alone.
- However, if a court was satisfied that a child was suffering or likely to suffer 'significant harm' it could impose an order which would authorise the child's removal (see emergency protection order).
- The NSPCC suggests that no child of under thirteen years of age should be left unsupervised for more than brief periods.

Medical Treatment

- If of 'sufficient understanding to make an informed decision', a child or young person of any age may give a valid consent to treatment [Gillick v West Norfolk & Wisbech Health Authority [1985] 3 All ER 402].
- This does not give them the right to refuse treatment and a child/young person could not for example override consent given by someone who has parental responsibility for them or by a court.

Name Change

- A child/young person of any age can, if thought to understand the implications, change their name by signing a 'statutory declaration'.
- If subject of a 'residence order' or a 'care order' a child's name cannot be changed without either the consent of everyone who has parental responsibility or a court [ss.13 & 33(7) Children Act 1989].

Passport

- A child/young person of any age must have a passport of their own [Internationally Agreed Convention].

- Children on a parent's passport as at October 5 1998 will not be affected until it is due for renewal, or the child reaches sixteen years of age.

Police Powers of Protection

- A child/young person of any age can be made subject of 'police powers of protection' (which allow a constable to remove and accommodate her/him or ensure that s/he remains where s/he is) if:

  - The police believe that the child/young person would otherwise suffer 'significant harm' [s.46 Children Act 1989]

Premium Bonds

- A child/young person of any age can have premium bonds in their name [Government Policy]

Prohibited Steps Order (see also s.8 Order)

- If a court is satisfied that s/he has sufficient understanding a child/young person of any age may be given leave (i.e permission) to make an application for a 'prohibited steps order'.

- A prohibited steps order prevents any person from taking any step which could be taken by a parent in meeting their parental responsibility for a child [s.10 Children Act 1989].

Religion

- A child/young person of any age who can make an informed decision may choose their own religion.
- Those who have parental responsibility could, if they believed that the choice would be harmful eg. so as to prevent them coming under the influence of undesirable sects, apply for a 'prohibited steps order' (see index) or seek to make the child/young person a ward of the High Court.

Residence Order (see also s.8 Order)

- If a court is satisfied that s/he has sufficient understanding a child/young person of any age may be given leave (ie. permission) to make an application for a 'residence order' [s.10 Children Act 1989].
- A residence order under s.8 Children Act 1989 will determine with whom the child/young person is to live.

s.8 (Children Act 1989) Orders (see also Contact, Prohibited Steps, Residence and Specific Issue Orders)

- If a court is satisfied that s/he has sufficient understanding a child/young person of any age may be given leave (i.e. permission) to make an application for any of the four sorts of section 8 Order introduced by the Children Act 1989 [s.10 Children Act 1989].

Smoking

- A child/young person of any age can smoke although under sixteen year olds can have their tobacco confiscated by police (or indeed a park keeper in uniform) if they are found smoking in any street or public place [s.7 Children & Young Persons Act 1933].

Specific Issue Order (see also s.8 Orders)

- If a court is satisfied that s/he has sufficient understanding a child/young person of any age may be given leave (ie. permission) to make an application for a 'specific issue order' [s.10 Children Act 1989].

- A specific issue order under s.8 Children Act 1989 resolves a particular problem eg. choice of schooling or need for medical treatment).

From Age 5

Alcohol

- A five year old may drink alcohol in private premises eg. at home [s.5 Children & Young Persons Act 1933].
- If a child is harmed by a parent or other person giving a child alcohol that person may be charged with a criminal offence.

Cinema

- An unaccompanied child of five can generally see a U or PG certificate film (though in London s/he may be required to be seven).

Fares

- A child's fare is payable for those of five or over when travelling on:
  - Trains
  - Buses and Tube trains in London [Conditions of Carriage London Transport]
  - Buses in most other parts of England and Wales

School Attendance

- A child who has reached the age of five must receive full-time education [s.8 (2) Education Act 1996].
- Parent/s are obliged to ensure that their children of compulsory school age receive efficient full-time education whether by regular attendance at school or otherwise [s.7 Education Act 1996].

Truants – Power to Remove

- If a police officer finds a school age child of five years or over in a public place and has reasonable grounds for believing that the child is truanting, s/he can remove the child/young person and place her/him in school or in another designated premises [s.16 Crime and Disorder Act 1998]

From Age 7

Savings / Current Account

- A child of seven and over can operate a National Savings or Trustee Savings Bank account [Policy Positions].
- A bank may allow a seven year old to operate an account if it is satisfied that s/he fully understands what s/he is doing.

From Age 10

Action Plan Order

- A child/young person of ten and over may, if not already subject to one of a number of other court orders, be made subject of an 'action plan order'
- An action plan order compels the offender for a period of three months to meet a series of requirements as to activity, location and reparation [ss.69-72 Powers of Criminal Courts (Sentencing) Act 2000].

Anti-Social Behaviour Order

- An 'anti-social behaviour order' may be made on a child of ten or over if :
  - S/he has acted in a manner that caused or was likely to cause harassment, alarm or distress to one or more persons, not of the same household as her/himself and
  - Such an order is necessary to protect persons within the Local Authority area [s.1 Crime & Disorder Act 1998]

Attendance Centre

- If found guilty of an offence for which an adult could be imprisoned, a child of ten and over may be ordered to attend a junior attendance centre for a maximum of twenty four hours [s.60 Powers of Criminal Courts (Sentencing) Act 2000].

Criminal Liability

- A child of less than ten cannot be convicted of a criminal offence.
- A child of less than ten who behaves in a way which could lead to prosecution of a child of ten or over might be considered 'likely to suffer significant harm' because

s/he is beyond parental control and thus be placed under the supervision of or in the care of the Local Authority by a court (see Supervision and Care Orders in index).

- The 'child safety order' (see index) might also be considered for such a child.

NB. The presumption of an inability amongst ten to thirteen year olds to distinguish right from wrong was abolished by s.34 Crime & Disorder Act 1998.

Curfew Order

- A child of ten and over may be made subject by a court of a 'curfew order' requiring her/him to remain for a specified time at a specified place (usually home) [ss.37-40 Powers of Criminal Courts (Sentencing) Act 2000].

NB. For ten to fifteen year olds, the maximum duration of this order is three months, and for sixteen and seventeen year olds, six.

Detention During Her Majesty's Pleasure

- If found guilty of murder a child/young person of ten or over may be detained indefinitely 'during Her Majesty's pleasure' [s.90 Powers of Criminal Courts (Sentencing) Act 2000].

Detention for a Specified Period

- A child/young person of ten to seventeen, if found guilty of:
    - An offence which in the case of a person aged twenty one or over carries a sentence of fourteen years or more (other than one for which the sentence is fixed)
    - Indecent assault on a woman
    - Indecent assault on a man committed after September 30 1999

    may be sentenced to a period of detention not exceeding the maximum allowable in the case of a person aged twenty one or over [s.91 (1);(3) Powers of Criminal Courts (Sentencing) Act 2000].

Police Detention

- If arrested and detained by the police a child of ten and over can:
    - Be searched (including strip searched) and/or an intimate search of body orifices undertaken by a doctor or a registered nurse
    - Be fingerprinted
    - Photographed
    - Asked to provide non-intimate body samples eg. hair or saliva

- Intimate samples eg. blood or semen will require parental consent if child is less than fourteen and the young person's and parent's if s/he is fourteen or over).

- A parent must be informed of the arrest/detention of a child/young person who has the right to communicate privately with a solicitor or inform someone else of their arrest, and to remain silent.

- The child/young person should only be interviewed when a parent or other responsible person who is not a police officer is present [Police & Criminal Evidence Act 1984, Criminal Justice and Police Act 2001 and Current Code of Practice].

Rape / Unlawful Sexual Intercourse

- A boy of ten and over may be charged with rape, attempted rape or unlawful sexual intercourse with a girl under sixteen [s.1 Sexual Offences Amendment Act 1993].

Referral Order

- A child/young person of ten or over upon conviction, must or may be referred to a 'youth offender panel' according to the crimes s/he has committed and the circumstances.

- The youth offender panel will arrange a suitable behaviour contract with the child/young person [Part III Powers of Criminal Courts (Sentencing) Act 2000].

Remands to Local Authority Accommodation

- Defendants of ten to sixteen inclusive, if refused bail can be remanded to accommodation which the local authority is obliged to provide [s.23 Children and Young Person's Act 1969 as substituted by s.60.Criminal Justice Act 1991].

Supervision Order (Criminal)

- If found guilty of a criminal offence a child of ten to seventeen inclusive may be made subject of a criminal 'supervision order' lasting up to three years [s.63 Powers of Criminal Courts (Sentencing) Act 2000].

Work

- A child of ten or over may, if local bye-laws say so, be employed on an occasional basis by a parent (who has to provide direct supervision), to do light agricultural/horticultural work [s.18(2) & s.20(2) Children and Young Person's Act 1933 as amended].

Youth Court

- The Magistrates Court which deals with juvenile crime is known as the Youth Court and has jurisdiction over ten to seventeen year olds inclusive [ss.68;70 & Sch.8 Criminal Justice Act 1991].

From Age Twelve

Cinema

- A child of twelve and over may watch a '12 Certificate' film.

Performance

- If the Local Authority grant her/him a licence a child of twelve and over may be trained to participate in dangerous performances [s.24 Children & Young Person's Act 1933].

NB. The maximum numbers of continuous hours per day any child (of nine or over) may rehearse or participate in a performance is nine [The Children (Performances) (Amendment) (no.2) Regulations 2000].

Pet Purchase

- A child of twelve and over may purchase a pet [s.3 Pet Animals Act 1951].

Remands to Secure Accommodation

- A court can, if certain criteria are satisfied, remand to secure accommodation to be provided by the Local Authority:
  - Boys or girls aged twelve to fourteen
  - Girls aged fifteen or sixteen

[s.23(4) Children and Young Persons' Act 1969 as substituted by Criminal Justice Act 1991 and amended by s.97(1) Crime and Disorder Act 1998].

From Age Thirteen

Secure Accommodation

- A child of thirteen to seventeen inclusive who is 'looked after' by a Local Authority can, if certain criteria are met, be placed in a children's home which provides secure accommodation [s.25 Children Act 1989].

- A child of under thirteen cannot be placed in secure accommodation without the permission of the Secretary of State for Health and Social Services [The Children (Secure Accommodation) Regulations 1991 as amended].

Work

- A child of thirteen may undertake 'light' work only in jobs specified in local bye-laws for not more than one hour before school [s.18 Children and Young Person's Act 1933 as amended and the Children (Protection at Work) Regulations 1998].

- Bye-laws (ie. made by local Authorities) are likely to specify 'permitted' employment as:

  - Agricultural/horticultural work
  - Newspaper delivery
  - Shop work including shelf stocking
  - Hairdressing salons

- Car washing by hand in a private residential setting
- Cafes
- Riding stables
- Domestic work in hotels

■ A Local Authority is also empowered to make bye-laws which:
- Distinguish between children of different ages, sexes, localities, trades, occupation and circumstances
- Prohibit specified occupations
- Prescribe minimum ages and numbers of hours in each day or week and times for which a child may be employed as well as meals and rest intervals and holidays plus other conditions

■ 'Light work' is work not likely to be harmful to safety or health and development of children or affect school attendance or ability to learn.

■ 'Prohibited employment' is likely to be defined by Local Authorities to include delivering milk, collecting money, work more than three metres above the ground, amusement arcades and personal care in residential care and nursing homes (unless under supervision of a responsible adult).

From Age Fourteen

Attendance Centre

- If found guilty of an offence for which an adult could be imprisoned, those aged fourteen and over may be ordered to attend an attendance centre for a minimum of twelve hours and a maximum of twenty four (which rises to thirty six hours for those over sixteen years of age) [s.60 Powers of Criminal Courts (Sentencing) Act 2000].

Detention for a Specified Period

- A young person of fourteen to seventeen convicted for causing death by reckless driving or causing death by careless driving while under the influence of drink or drugs may receive a fixed sentence of detention up the maximum allowable for a person aged twenty one or over [s.91 (2);(3) Powers of Criminal Courts (Sentencing) Act 2000].

Seatbelts

- A young person of fourteen and over is personally responsible for ensuring that (where they are fitted and must be worn) they use a seat belt [s.14 Road Traffic

Act 1988 & Motor Vehicles (Wearing of Seat Belts) Regulations 1993].

Pubs

- A young person of fourteen to seventeen inclusive may enter a pub but must not buy or drink alcohol [s.169 Licensing Act 1964].

Work

- A child of fourteen or over may be employed (for light work only, paid or unpaid) outside of school hours:
  - For two hours or less between 7am - 7pm on school days and Sundays (and a maximum of twelve hours in a school week)
  - For up to five hours in any day which is not a school day or Sunday
  - For up to twenty five hours per week in any week in which s/he is not required to attend school

  so long as s/he has a rest break of one hour every four hours and a break of two consecutive weeks during a period in the year when not required to attend school.

- A fourteen year old may only engage in street trading if employed by her/his parent, directly supervised by them and licensed by the Local Authority [s.18 Children and Young Persons' Act 1933 as amended and Children (Protection at Work) Regulations 1998].

NB. *'Light work' is work not likely to be harmful to safety or health or development of children or affect school attendance or ability to learn.*

'Prohibited employment' is likely to be defined by Local Authorities to include delivering milk, collecting money, work more than three metres above the ground, amusement arcades and personal care in residential care and nursing homes (unless under supervision of a responsible adult).

From Age Fifteen

Cinema

- A young person of fifteen or over can see a '15 Certificate' film at a cinema.

Detention and Training Order

- A young person of fifteen to seventeen found guilty of an offence for which a person aged twenty one or over could be imprisoned, may be sentenced to a minimum of four and a maximum of twenty four months 'detention and training order' [s.101(1);(2) Powers of Criminal Courts (Sentencing) Act 2000].

Work

- A child/young person of fifteen may be employed (light work only) outside of school hours:
  - For two hours or less between 7am – 7pm on school days and Sundays (and for a maximum of twelve hours in a school week)
  - For up to eight hours a day on any day which is not a school day or Sunday;
  - For up to thirty five hours per week in any week in s/he is not required to attend school

  so long as s/he has a rest break of one hour every four hours, a break of two consecutive weeks during a period in the year when not required to attend school [s.18 Children & Young Person's Act 1933 as amended and the Children (Protection at Work) Regulations 1998].

NB. *'Light work' is work not likely to be harmful to safety or health or development of children or affect school attendance or ability to learn.*

'Prohibited employment' is likely to be defined by Local Authorities to include delivering milk, collecting money, work more than three metres above the ground, amusement arcades and personal care in residential care or nursing homes (unless under supervision of a responsible adult).

From Age Sixteen

Alcohol

- A young person of sixteen may, in a pub or hotel for consumption with a meal, drink (but not buy), beer, porter or cider (but not spirits or wine) [s.169 Licensing Act 1964].

Armed Forces

- A young person (of either sex) can (with parental consent) join the Armed Forces when s/he is sixteen [Queen's Regulations as amended].

Community Service Order

- If found guilty of an offence for which an adult could be imprisoned a young person of sixteen may be made subject of a 'community service order' requiring her/him to do specified unpaid work [s.46 Powers of Criminal Courts (Sentencing) Act 2000].

Cruelty to Child

- A young person of sixteen may be charged with cruelty to a child of whom they have actual care [s.1 Children & Young Person's Act 1933].

Dental Treatment

- Unless in full-time education a young person of sixteen may be charged for certain dental treatment [National Health Service (Travelling and Remission of Charges) Regulations 1988].

Driving Licence

- A sixteen year old can hold a licence to drive a moped, mowing machine, tractor, invalid carriage or pedestrian controlled vehicle [s.101 Road Traffic Act 1988 & Motor Vehicle (Driving Licences) Regulations 1987].

Fares

- A sixteen year old is liable for full fares on buses and trains and on London tube trains [Conditions of Carriage (London Transport)]

Gliding

- At sixteen a young person can be a pilot in command of a glider [Article 31 Air Navigation Order 2000].

Heterosexual Intercourse

- A young woman of sixteen can lawfully consent to vaginal or anal intercourse with a man [the net effect of ss.5;6 &12 & sch.2 Sexual Offences Act 1956, s.2 & sch.2 para.14 Criminal Law Act 1967 & s.1 Sexual Offences Act (Amendment) Act 2000].

NB. A boy or girl under sixteen is not committing a criminal offence if s/he has intercourse with a male or female who is sixteen or over and consents. However, the older person could be prosecuted for indecent assault and in certain circumstances also be guilty of 'an abuse of a position of trust' (see index).

Homelessness

- A young person of sixteen or seventeen may in certain circumstances be entitled to accommodation from their local authority because either:

    - They are in 'priority need' as a result of pregnancy, having a dependant child or are otherwise vulnerable eg. as a result of a learning

disability [s.59 Housing Act 1985 and Homelessness Code of Guidance for Local Authorities 1991] or
- They are assessed as 'in need' and that their welfare would be seriously damaged without accommodation being provided [s.20(3) Children Act 1989].

■ A young person of sixteen or seventeen has an explicit right to overrule a parent who wishes to resume her/his care.

Homosexual Intercourse

■ A young man or woman aged sixteen or over can lawfully consent to homosexual acts (including anal intercourse) [s.1 Sexual Offences (Amendment) Act 2000].

NB. A boy or girl under sixteen is not committing a criminal offence if s/he has intercourse with a male or female who is sixteen or over and consents. However, the older person could be prosecuted for indecent assault and in certain circumstances also be guilty of 'an abuse of a position of trust' (see index).

Leaving Care

- Any young person aged sixteen to twenty one (twenty four if in full-time education or training) who has been 'looked after' for a minimum of three months since their fourteenth birthday, is entitled to have their needs assessed and met by the Local Authority who last looked after them [s.1 Children (Leaving Care) Act 2000].

Leaving Home

- A sixteen or seventeen year old can leave home without parental consent but might be prevented:
  - In the case of a sixteen year old by means of a successful application by the Local Authority for a care order or
  - In the case of a sixteen or seventeen year old by being made a 'Ward of the High Court' [s.41 Supreme Court Act 1991].

Marriage

- A young person of sixteen can marry :
  - With the consent of both parents (if they are married or if an unmarried father has parental responsibility) or

- If a residence order exists, with the consent of the holder of that order instead of the parent/s or
- If a care order exists, then with the consent of the relevant Local Authority as well as that of the parent/s [s.3 Marriage Act 1949 as amended]

- If a young person of sixteen or seventeen marries without such consents the marriage is valid but they will have committed a criminal offence.

Medical Treatment

- A young person of sixteen may provide consent to surgical/medical/dental treatment and unless there are grounds for believing that s/he is mentally incompetent under the Mental Health Act 1983, no further consent is required [s.8 Family Law Reform Act 1969].

- This does not give them the right to refuse treatment. They could not for example override consent given by someone who has parental responsibility for them or by a court.

NB. Consent to surgical/medical/dental treatment does not extend to the donation of blood or body organs.

Name Change

- A sixteen year old can record a new name by filing a deed poll with the High Court.

Optical Treatment

- A sixteen year old may be charged for both an eye test and optical treatment unless:
  - In full-time education
  - Any member of family is in receipt of income support
  - Income is low or
  - Eyesight is constantly changing [National Health Service (Optical Charges & Payments) Regulations 1989]

Passport

- Subject to written consent of a parent a sixteen year old can apply for a passport themselves. They can no longer travel on a parent's passport [Internationally Agreed Convention].
- A parent's consent in unnecessary if the young person is married, or in the Armed Forces [Queen's Regulations].

Performance

- A sixteen year old can without a local authority licence:
  - Participate in public performances or
  - Train to take part in dangerous performances [s.37 Children & Young Person's Act 1933]

Prescription Charges

- A sixteen year old may be charged with the cost of prescriptions unless:
  - In full-time education
  - Pregnant
  - In receipt of income support/family credit
  - On a low income or
  - In certain other limited circumstances [National Health Service (Charges for Drugs and Appliances) Regulations 1980].

Probation Order

- At sixteen a young person may be made subject of a Probation Order which can last from six months to three years [s.41 Powers of Criminal Courts (Sentencing) Act 2000].

School Attendance

- A young person who is sixteen during the school year (ie. including the summer holidays) can legally leave school on the last Friday in June [s.8 Education Act 1996].

- In practice, if their GCSEs finish earlier, the Head Teacher has discretion to allow a pupil to leave before this date.

Smoking

- A sixteen year old may lawfully buy cigarettes, tobacco and cigarette papers [s.7 Children & Young Person's Act 1933].

Work

- A sixteen year old who has left school may work full-time (and obtain a national insurance number) [Education Act 1996].

- Everyone over school leaving age who works and has a contract of employment is entitled after three months, to four weeks paid holiday per [Working Time Regulations 1998].

From Age Seventeen

Blood Donation

- At seventeen a young person may donate her/his blood.
- This reflects the current policy of the Blood Transfusion Service.

Care Order

- At seventeen it is no longer possible for a court to make a care order.
- Where a child is sixteen or under and a court finds that s/he 'is suffering or likely to suffer significant harm', which is attributable to inadequate parental care or that the child is beyond parental control, they can make a care order which will mean that (potentially until the child/young person is eighteen) the Local Authority shares parental responsibility with parents and can decide where s/he shall live [s.31 Children Act 1989].

NB. A 'care order' cannot be made on a young person of sixteen who is or has been married.

Driving Licence

- At seventeen a young person may hold a driving licence to drive a:
  - Motorbike (with or without sidecar);
  - Three wheeler car, tricycle or van (up to a weight of 500KG);
  - Car or van with up to nine seats and maximum weight of 3,500KG;
  - Road-roller [s.101 Road Traffic Act 1988].

Flying

- A seventeen year old may obtain a private pilot's licence to fly a plane, gyro plane, helicopter, balloon or airship [Sch.8 Air Navigation Order 2000].

Supervision Order (Welfare)

- At seventeen it is no longer possible for a court to make a welfare supervision order.
- If a court finds that a child/young person of up to and including sixteen 'is suffering or likely to suffer significant harm', which is attributable to inadequate parental care they can make a supervision order to the Local Authority which will mean that for at least twelve months, the child/young person will be advised, assisted

and befriended and, together with their parent/current caregiver must comply with directions given by the supervising officer [s.31 Children Act 1989].

From Age 18

AN EIGHTEEN YEAR OLD HAS REACHED THE AGE OF MAJORITY AND BECOMES AN ADULT AS FAR AS THE LAW IS CONCERNED
[s.1 Family Law Reform Act 1969]

Abuse of Position of Trust

- A person aged eighteen or over can be prosecuted if s/he is in a 'position of trust' with respect to a person less than eighteen years of age and:
  - Has sexual intercourse with that person or
  - Engages in any other sexual activity with or directed towards that person [s.3 Sexual Offences (Amendment) Act 2000]
- A person is in a 'position of trust' if s/he looks after (ie. regularly involved in caring for, training, supervising or being in sole charge of) a person:
  - Detained in an institution as a result of a court order or legal power
  - Resident in a children's home

- Care for in a hospital or care home
- Receiving full-time education at a n educational institution [s.4 Sexual Offences (Amendment) Act 2000]

NB. This law is intended to protect vulnerable young people from exploitation. It is a defence if the older person can satisfy the court s/he did not know the younger person was less than eighteen, or that s/he was in a 'position of trust', or that s/he was lawfully married to the younger person.

Adoption

- A person of eighteen years of age or over cannot be adopted.
- Someone who has been adopted can:
  - Apply to the Registrar General for a copy of her/his original birth certificate [s.51 Adoption Act 1976]
  - Apply to place their name and address on the adoption contact register [s.51A Adoption Act 1976]

Alcohol

- At eighteen a young person may buy and consume alcohol in a pub or a bar [s.169 Licensing Act 1964].

NB. A person aged less than eighteen commits no offence if s/he tries to buy alcohol at the request of police or weights and measures officers ie. has been engaged to test the responses of local off-licences and pubs etc.

Armed Forces

- At eighteen a young person can join the Armed Forces without parental consent.

Betting

- An eighteen year old can enter a betting shop and place a bet [s.21 Betting, Gaming and Lotteries Act 1963].
- An under eighteen year old is allowed to enter a bingo club so long as s/he does not participate in a game.

Cinema

- At eighteen a young person may see an 'eighteen' rated film.

Contracts

- An eighteen year old may enter contractual arrangements and thus:
  - Buy property;
  - Sue and be sued;
  - Act as an executor / administrator of the estate of a dead person.

Dental Treatment

- An eighteen year old can be charged for dental treatment unless still in full-time education or pregnant [National Health Service (Travelling Expenses and Remission of Charges) Regulations 1988].

Driving Licence

- At eighteen a young person may hold a licence to drive a goods vehicle of up to 7.5 tonnes [s.101 Road Traffic Act 1988].

Fireworks

- A young person of eighteen may lawfully buy fireworks [s.31 Explosive Act 1875 & para.7 Fireworks (Safety) Regulations 1997].

NB. Caps, crackers, snaps, novelty matches, part-poppers, serpents and throw-downs can be supplied to young persons aged sixteen or seventeen according to the Department of Trade and Industry information leaflets.

Flying

- A young person of eighteen can obtain a commercial pilot's licence to fly a glider, aeroplane, helicopter, gyro plane, balloon or airship [Sch.8 Air Navigation Order 2000].

Hypnotism

- At eighteen a young person may participate in a hypnotic show [s.3 Hypnotism Act 1952]

Jury Service

- An eighteen year may serve on a jury [s.1 Juries Act 1974].

Minimum Wage

- Eighteen to twenty-one year olds inclusive are entitled to a minimum hourly rate which was £3.50 from October 1 2001 and is due to rise to £3-60 on October 1 2002 [s.1 Minimum Wages Act 1998].

Mortgage

- An eighteen year old may take out a mortgage.

Solvents

- It is an offence for a shop assistant to sell solvents to anyone under eighteen if it is considered the product may be abused by the person [s.1 Intoxicating Substances Supply Act 1985].
- It is also an offence to sell to under eighteen year old, gas lighter refills [s.11 Consumer Protection Act 1987].

Tattoo

- At eighteen a young person may be tattooed without parental consent [s.1 Tattooing of Minors Act 1969].

Tissue / Body Donation

- At eighteen a young person can, without parental consent:
  - Bequeath tissues for transplant purposes or;
  - Donate her/his body to medical science

Voting

- At eighteen a young person may vote in local, general and European elections [ss.1(1)(c) & 2(1)(c) Representation of the Peoples Act 1983].

Will

- An eighteen year old can make a valid will [s.7 Wills Act 1837].
- Special arrangements exist to enable under eighteen year olds who are in the Armed Forces to make a will [s.1 Wills (Soldiers and Sailors Act 1918].

From Age 21

Adoption

- At twenty one, it becomes possible to adopt a child [s.14 Adoption Act 1976]
- An 'adoption order' can be made in favour of a married couple (one of whom is the actual parent and at least eighteen) and the other twenty one years of age.

Councillor

- At twenty one, it is possible to become a local councillor [s.79 Local Government Act 1972].

Driving Licence

- A twenty one year old may hold a licence to drive a heavy goods or a large passenger vehicle [s.101 Road Traffic Act 1988].

Member of Parliament

- At twenty one, it is possible to become a Member of Parliament [s.7 Parliamentary Elections Act 1695].

Prison

- If given a custodial sentence a twenty one year old will be placed in prison rather than a young offenders' institution [effect of s.96 Powers of Criminal Courts (Sentencing) Act 2001].

Appendix 1 - Useful Organisations

CitizenCard

- Backed by the Home Office and Department of Health, 'Citizencard' issue to children aged six upwards and resident in the UK,' proof of age' cards.
- For further information call 0870 240 1221 or visit www.citizencard.net

Children's Legal Centre

- Gives expert legal advice to young people and has lots of simple information books and leaflets.
- Call 01206 873820 Monday to Friday 2-5pm and Wednesday 10am to 12 noon; write to CLC University of Essex, Wivenhoe Park, Colchester CO4 3SQ or email CLC@essex.ac.uk

Childline

- Offers a confidential help-line if you are worried or frightened or just need someone to talk to.
- Call (free) 24 hours a day 0800 1111

Message Home

- A national free-call help-line for those who have run away or left home so that they can send a message to their family or seek confidential help and advice.
- Call (free) 24 hours a day 0800 700740

Appendix 2 - Children Act Enterprises Publications

- Available from:

Children Act Enterprises
103 Mayfield Road
South Croydon
Surrey CR2 0BH

tel: 020 8651 0554; fax: 020 8405 8483
email: childact@dial.pipex.com

Personal Guides:

- The Human Fertilisation and Embryology Act 1990
- Children Act 1989 in The Context of The Human Rights Act 1998
- Childminding and Day Care (England)
- Childminding and Day Care (Northern Ireland)
- For Children and Young People Being Cared for By Social Services and Voluntary Organisations
- Residential Care of Children & Young People (England and Wales)
- 'How Old Do I Have To Be ?' (a simple guide to the rights and responsibilities of 0 - 21 year olds)
- Adoption Act 1976
- Domestic Violence (Part IV Family Law Act 1996 & Protection from Harassment Act 1997)
- Crime and Disorder Act 1998 In The Context of The Powers of Criminal Courts (Sentencing) Act 2000.
- Looking After Children: Good Parenting, Good Outcomes (DoH LAC System)
- Discounts for orders of 100 or more

See our web-page
http://ds.dial.pipex.com/childact

Notes

Notes

Notes

Notes

Notes

Notes

Notes

Notes

Notes

Notes

Notes